Contents

Introduction

Work is an important part of our lives. We rely on it for income, but many of us also want more. We expect work to be stimulating, to use our skills, and to fit in with our other commitments and interests.

We often seek a sense of moving forward in our working lives. This is what many people mean by the term 'career'. Some people get that sense of moving forward from pursuing quite conventional and structured careers, for example in established professions. Most of us, however, have to make our own careers by seeing what we might like to do and then finding ways of getting there. Our ideas and opportunities often change along the way. You can see your career as your own evolving story of your working life.

However, very few of us put much effort into planning for the kind of career we want. Thinking about where we are going at work is something we all need to do throughout our working lives.

The nature of work and employment is always changing. As the economy goes up and down it is obviously much easier at some times to gain access to your chosen work. When times are hard we need to be better at showing we have something special to offer and may need to be more flexible in our plans.

New kinds of jobs emerge all the time and many labour markets are becoming increasingly specialized. This means we need to find out more about the kinds of jobs which interest us, and we need to understand what employers are looking for and how people get these jobs.

Careers also operate differently in different countries. For example, how you ask for information or contact a potential employer needs to be approached in a way that fits the local culture.

Career planning is not something we need to do alone. You will see that there are many ways in which we can get help and support from other people. Technology is also putting huge amounts of job-related information within our reach. Social networking sites further extend the ways we can contact other people and talk about our career experiences and theirs too.

By working through a simple series of steps and exercises, you can help yourself to be clearer about what you want, what your options are, and how to move forward. If you want to use this book to go through these steps, you should begin by acquiring a notebook or folder in which to keep the information you will be generating. Exercises in each chapter will help you build this collection of information and reflect on what you are learning about yourself and the process of career planning as you go along.

We shall look at one step in this process of career planning on each day of the week:

Sunday What do you want from work?

Monday What kind of job would you enjoy?

Tuesday What are you good at?

Wednesday Identifying your career options

Thursday Collecting information

Friday Making choices

Saturday Taking the first steps

At the end of each chapter you will find two sets of questions. First, some multiple choice questions help you check your understanding. Each of these questions has one correct answer. Second, some deeper questions help you reflect on your own career planning progress. These do not have correct or incorrect answers! You might like to add these reflections to your notes from the exercises as you go along.

SUNDAY

What do you want from work?

In taking the first steps towards a new career plan, we look at the following issues:

● your motivation for planning
● a simple framework for career planning
● what you want from work

As we set out to consider what we are doing at work and where we wish to go, there are always a number of seemingly good reasons to put it off yet again. So we have to start by confronting why we need to look at our own careers, and what the likely benefits might be.

Even if we are convinced that we need to do some career planning, it can seem hard to know where to start. That is where a simple framework helps. It cuts up a complex activity into smaller pieces we can tackle.

Today also includes your first real task – considering what you really want from work, in terms of how your work needs to fit with your personal values and lifestyle preferences.

Clearing away the barriers

The very term 'career' often seems daunting. It can help to think of a career simply as a sequence of work experiences. These can involve sideways moves, moves between employers and/or between different types of work, and even periods out of paid employment. Some people are having 'portfolio' careers, combining several paid or unpaid work activities at the same time. However, all careers need thinking about if we are to find satisfaction in our work and non-work lives.

A barrier to career planning for many people is the lack of a clear approach to thinking their way through the many uncertainties involved in sorting out future job options. We will introduce a simple framework which can be used to guide our thinking.

Once you have looked at why you need to plan, and have understood the overall framework, then you are ready to move on to the first personal task: to take a long cool look at what you really want to get out of work.

The aim of these initial steps is to reduce your level of anxiety and set you free to think as widely as possible before you narrow down the field to particular jobs. Few of us are ever really lateral enough in our career planning.

Why try to plan your career?

Most of us feel from time to time that we should reconsider where we are going, but it seems safer not to think about it just yet.

Career planning is not just for the very young or the redundant. Most of us will need to rethink our careers several times in our working lives. Indeed, how we manage our working lives in middle age and beyond is becoming one of the most exciting and challenging issues of our times.

Such rethinking may lead to very modest changes, such as a rather different job with your current employer. Or it may lead to a much more radical change of direction, as you realize that the essence of your line of work does not suit or satisfy you. Or it may result in no change at all, except a new appreciation of where you are going and why it feels right.

Planning as a necessity

It is important to be aware that by not planning you put yourself in real danger.

Work opportunities are changing all the time, and some jobs become obsolete or reduce in numbers as others open up. If we do not ensure our own employability by acquiring the right skills and moving into areas which offer some opportunity, then no one else will do it for us.

Gone are the days when careers were an orderly progression managed by the employer. These days change is continuous. Work often comes as projects and most employers expect individual employees to take the main responsibility for managing their own careers. This means we must look around for suitable work avenues to pursue and persuade our employers that we are ready to tackle fresh challenges.

If you are in any real doubt as to whether you should stop and think about your career direction, remember that 'failing to plan is planning to fail'. Successful people often say they have 'just been lucky'. This is true only to the extent that none of us can map out our future careers in every detail. Success, however, does depend on having some goals in mind and seeking opportunities to move towards them.

Your own reasons for reviewing your career

Now you need to clarify why you are looking at your career at this particular time. Some reasons might be:

- trying to get into work for the first time
- not enjoying your current job (finding it boring, stressful, frustrating, etc.)
- feeling that you are being poorly managed by your current boss or that management generally is not good in your organization
- feeling that career progression is blocked (no obvious next step, employer does not recognize potential, etc.)

- suspicion that you are in the wrong kind of work altogether and need a more radical change
- fear of job loss, or wish to maintain employability
- trying to find a new route back into paid work (after redundancy, an educational course, illness or a period of caring for dependants)
- wondering how best to manage the transition from work to retirement
- a desire for other forms of work (voluntary work, work in 'retirement', self-employment, etc.)
- wishing to find a better fit between work and non-work priorities (caring for children, less travelling, more flexible or shorter hours).

You might well have more than one reason for wanting to think about your career at this time. Jot them in your notebook.

A framework for career planning

Any approach to career planning involves focusing both on yourself and on the job market. The framework used here encourages you to think first about yourself.

First consider three main questions in relation to yourself:

- What do you want from work? (work values)
- What kind of job would you enjoy? (job interests)
- What are you good at? (skills)

Then turn your attention to the **job market** and:

- look at the broad types of jobs available
- identify some possible career options
- find out about jobs with which you are not familiar, either inside your organization or elsewhere.

On the firm foundation of these two types of knowledge you can then:

- make your career choices
- start to take action on your skills and job hunting.

A simple diagram can help you to remember these basic building blocks of career planning. You can see that your preparation in terms of learning about yourself and jobs supports your ability to plan your career and make choices in an informed way.

The building blocks of career planning

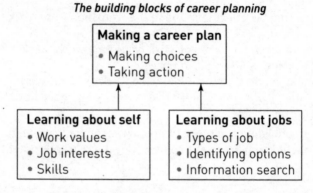

Making a career plan
- Making choices
- Taking action

Learning about self
- Work values
- Job interests
- Skills

Learning about jobs
- Types of job
- Identifying options
- Information search

As you undertake activities – like those suggested in this book – you are 'doing' career planning. But at the same time, you need to keep reflecting to gain a deeper understanding, especially about yourself and ways of thinking about your work and career that seem most helpful for you. Throughout the book we will talk about 'doing' and 'reflecting' in career planning to encourage the habit of always following an exercise or practical activity with a short period of reflection.

As you work on your career plan, both the 'doing' and 'reflecting' are helping you to develop career planning skills you can use and improve throughout your life. These skills include keeping a positive view of yourself even when things are not going well, interacting effectively with other people (e.g. when asking for some help), knowing how to find information on work and learning opportunities, and taking career decisions in a calm and balanced way.

What do you want to get out of work?

The rest of today's programme will be devoted to starting to look at what you really want from work: your *work values*.

You may feel you work primarily to pay the bills. However, if you had to choose between two similar jobs, would you automatically take the job which paid more? Not necessarily. One job might involve a longer journey to work, the other might be in an organization you know to be facing an uncertain future.

It is clear that what would matter most to another person might not matter most to you. Some of us are happy to take a risky career decision, because, for instance, we are confident in our own abilities, or because we think that a particular job is really worthwhile.

Start with your real priorities

Knowing the kind of work that would meet your real priorities means understanding your work values.

Start by completing Exercise 1.

Exercise 1: understanding your work values

Give each statement a score out of 10 using the scale below.

0 _____ 10

Not important to me   *Extremely important to me*

How important is it that your work:	Score	Value	Work involves:	Rank
1 Encourages accomplishment and achievement?		Achievement/ Challenge	Using your abilities; offering interest and challenge	....
2 Offers you steady employment and security?		Security/Stability	A comfortable work environment that is not stressful	....
3 Provides new and different experiences?		Variety	Meeting new people and many different projects	....
4 Requires you to take personal and financial risks?		Enterprise/Risk	Creating something new from scratch; coping with uncertainty	....
5 Provides good financial rewards and social status?		Economic status	High salary, occupational and social standing, prestige	....
6 Benefits the community or provides a service to others?		Altruism/Service	Concern for the welfare of others; contributing to society	....
7 Gives you the opportunity to use your initiative?		Autonomy	Being in control of your own work	....
8 Is in an organization that treats people fairly?		Equity	Concern for fairness and equality of opportunity at work	....
9 Is with colleagues that are easy to get along with?		Social	Friendly work environment	....
10 Offers opportunities to direct and influence people?		Influence	Opportunities to lead, manage and influence	....

Now identify which statement has been given the highest score and rank that statement 1, find the statement with the next highest score and rank that statement 2, and so on. The order in which the values are ranked shows us the kind of rewards we want from work. Values ranked highest tell us what we want most from our work and those ranked low are likely to be relatively unimportant to us.

Where does work fit with the rest of your life?

This is another key question to think about early in the career planning process. For example, how much time do you want to devote to work? It is not just a question of whether you want to work full-time or part-time, or whether you mind working shifts or at weekends. The question is about how central you want your work to be in your life. How will you achieve work/life balance?

How important is it that you:

- have opportunities to work as a 'volunteer' for a charity or in a political campaign?
- spend time with your family and friends?
- are involved in caring for children or elderly parents?
- play sport or participate in your favourite hobby?

Perhaps it does not matter if your work takes over the whole of your life, because what you plan to do is going to be so important to you.

Many people seem to be more content with their overall work/life balance if they have some flexibility in hours, patterns or location of work. Consider how important such flexibility is to you now. Is this likely to change over the next few years?

It is not for ever

We all change, and our circumstances change. You are not committing yourself irreversibly to a course of action when you make career plans.

If you no longer want to continue with the sort of work you have been doing, it does not mean you were wrong to start doing this sort of work in the first place.

What matters most to someone at the age of 20 is not necessarily going to be what matters most to the same person at the age of 30 or 40. On the other hand, there may be things that you have always wanted to do or to try out but, for some reason, in the past have never had the opportunity to do or never thought it would be possible for them to be the basis of paid employment.

It is not too late

It may not be easy to change career direction, especially if it means leaving a well-paid secure job to start again at the bottom rung of a career ladder, or becoming a student again; but lots of people have done it.

Summary

We have spent Sunday examining the crucial issue of what we want from work. In doing that we have looked at:

- the barriers to career planning
- why you need to plan your career
- your own reasons for reviewing your career
- a framework for career planning
- understanding your work values
- where work fits with the rest of your life

We have seen that a career can take many forms and is not by any means an orderly progression up some pre-determined ladder. As labour markets become more complex we all have to take more responsibility for finding the kind of work that will satisfy our needs and preferences. This is what career planning is about.

The framework we will use for career planning in this book starts with two main foundations: learning about yourself and learning about jobs. On these foundations your career plan will rest. Career planning involves making some choices and then taking career action. Action can include improving your skills as well as looking for a job move or work experience.

SUNDAY

MONDAY

TUESDAY

WEDNESDAY

THURSDAY

FRIDAY

SATURDAY

You have made a start by examining your work values: the things that matter most to you. You have also considered how you wish your work to fit with the rest of your life, especially your outside interests and caring responsibilities.

Over the next six days we will work through the remaining six steps in planning your career. We continue on Monday by looking at job interests.

Questions

SUNDAY

MONDAY

TUESDAY

WEDNESDAY

THURSDAY

FRIDAY

SATURDAY

Questions to check your understanding

1. Career planning helps us to:
a) Work out exactly what our career should look like ❏
b) Avoid change ❏
c) Have some goals in mind and seek opportunities to move towards them ❏
d) Make our personal lives fit around our work ❏

2. Your career is:
a) What you do to get promoted ❏
b) The sequence of work experiences you have over time ❏
c) The plan you have for your future ❏
d) The periods when you are working full-time for a major employer ❏

3. Your work values are:
a) What makes you valuable to an employer ❏
b) What other people think you are good at ❏
c) The kinds of jobs you would find interesting ❏
d) What matters to you about work ❏

Questions to capture your reflections

1. What are the most important reasons you have for wishing to review your career at this time?
2. Which aspects of the career planning framework are you keen to explore?
3. Are there any aspects of career planning that you find rather daunting and so tend to avoid? Why do you think this is?
4. Which work values are most important to you? Did any of your reactions surprise you when you completed the values exercise?
5. Are there any values on the list that you know are not at all important to you?
6. What are the things outside work you want to have time for? Do these place any constraints on your work choices?
7. What do you hope to get out of the effort you put into the material covered in this book?

MONDAY

What kind of job would you enjoy?

Jobs differ in a wide variety of ways. Today we focus on trying to identify the sort of work that you would find interesting. Forget whether you have the skills, the knowledge, or even the experience; concentrate on finding out what kinds of work you would enjoy.

In doing this you are continuing with the process of learning about yourself. This is the essential first step to career planning. You may feel you already have a pretty good idea of what your interests are, but even if this is the case, there are several reasons why it is worth spending some time reviewing your interests. In particular, it is possible that those interests may have changed since you last thought about them. It is also helpful to be able to articulate your interests, especially when you start getting interviews for jobs. One of the favourite questions of job interviewers is, 'Why are you interested in this job?'

The map of work interests

Having got some idea about what is important to you, you need to start thinking about the direction in which you want to go. However, when embarking on any journey a map is required to show us what is out there. It is just the same when planning a career, although in this case several maps are required. Today, we are going to be looking at the first of these maps. This map is called **work interests.**

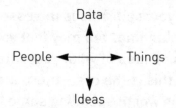

The first thing to do with any map is to orient it, and to do this we need a compass. The four points of the compass on the map of work interests are data, ideas, people and things.

The contents of jobs vary in many ways but some of the most fundamental differences concern whether they involve dealing with people, things, data or ideas. Of course, many types of work combine these four elements in varying proportions.

How to use the map

This map of work interests has several uses. First of all, if you are currently working, you can try to locate yourself, that is, to find out in what area of the map you are now. On the other hand, if you are not working, you need to find out where you were on the map when you last worked or studied. You also need to decide whether this is where you want to be or whether you really want to be somewhere else. Where would you like to be in an ideal world?

Once you have some firm ideas about where you want to be, you need to find out what sort of work opportunities exist there.

The problem is that there are so many jobs, and even the same job can seem quite different in one setting from how it feels in another. At this stage you are only trying to identify the territory in which you would like to be. Tomorrow you will have to determine whether you have, or can develop, the skills to survive there.

Establishing preferences: types of work activity

To help you determine what your work interests are, carry out the two exercises that follow. These look at interests in relation to six different types of work activity that combine a focus on people, things, data and ideas in various ways. The activities are:

- Entrepreneurial – activities found in business and management work
- Administrative – activities found in administrative and organizational work
- Practical – activities found in technical and practical work
- Intellectual – activities found in scientific and research work
- Creative – activities found in artistic and creative work
- Social – activities found in social and personal services work

The diagram shows how these six sorts of work activities relate to the two dimensions of our map: people – things and data – ideas.

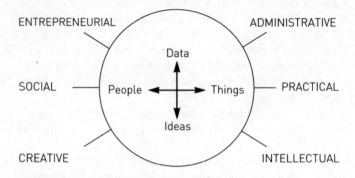

Exercise 2: your work interests

For the six sets of statements set out below, ask yourself: 'How interested am I in work that involves...'

Circle one number alongside each activity using the scale from 1 = no interest to 5 = strong interest.

Entrepreneurial (data/people)	
1 2 3 4 5	Persuading and influencing other people
1 2 3 4 5	Making business decisions
1 2 3 4 5	Managing/leading people
1 2 3 4 5	Taking business and financial risks
1 2 3 4 5	Getting people interested/involved in a project
Administrative (data/things)	
1 2 3 4 5	Creating systems or procedures for an office
1 2 3 4 5	Setting up a computer database
1 2 3 4 5	Working with figures
1 2 3 4 5	Getting all the details right
1 2 3 4 5	Clear structure and routine

Practical (things)					
1	2	3	4	5	Working with tools/machinery
1	2	3	4	5	Fixing and repairing things
1	2	3	4	5	Good hand-eye coordination
1	2	3	4	5	Working outside
1	2	3	4	5	Developing practical skills
Intellectual (ideas/things)					
1	2	3	4	5	Understanding/being curious
1	2	3	4	5	Researching/analysing information
1	2	3	4	5	Asking questions
1	2	3	4	5	Solving problems in your own way
1	2	3	4	5	Learning about new things
Creative (people/ideas)					
1	2	3	4	5	Using your imagination/expressing your ideas
1	2	3	4	5	Designing and making things
1	2	3	4	5	Performing/participating in artistic activities
1	2	3	4	5	Writing about films, plays, music or books
1	2	3	4	5	Working alongside creative people
Social (people)					
1	2	3	4	5	Teaching people
1	2	3	4	5	Helping people with their problems
1	2	3	4	5	Meeting and talking to people
1	2	3	4	5	Building relationships with people
1	2	3	4	5	Looking after and caring for people

Add up the score for each set of items (maximum score for
each area is 25). Then list in your notebook the six types of
activity in rank order from rank 1 for the highest-scoring set of
items to rank 6 for the lowest.

TINKER, TAILOR, SYSTEMS ANALYST...

Patterns of scores may vary in lots of different ways. You may score much higher on one or two of the interest areas than on the others. Alternatively, you may find that you seem to score highly in nearly all areas, or not score very highly in any area.

Before we go on to explore the meaning of this interests' profile, let's complete another exercise. This is a different way of looking at the same six types of work activity.

Exercise 3: preference for work activities
The purpose of this exercise is to examine your preferences for the six types of work activity.

Circle the type of activity you prefer in each pair:		
Practical *or* Creative	Creative *or* Social	Social *or* Administrative
Social *or* Entrepreneurial	Entrepreneurial *or* Intellectual	Intellectual *or* Social
Intellectual *or* Administrative	Administrative *or* Practical	Practical *or* Intellectual

Practical *or* Social	Creative *or* Intellectual	Entrepreneurial *or* Administrative
Creative *or* Entrepreneurial	Entrepreneurial *or* Practical	Administrative *or* Creative

Count up the number of times you have circled each type of activity and record the scores in your notebook. The maximum possible score for each type is 5. If you have counted correctly, when you add up all your scores they should total 15.

Now compare the three highest-scoring activity areas in the two exercises:

	Exercise 2	**Exercise 3**
Highest		*Intellectual*
Second		*Practical*
Third		

What do the results of the two exercises show? Have you identified the same work interest areas in both exercises as being of most importance to you?

Do your results show that you have one or two particularly strong areas of interest, or are several of your scores from these exercises similar?

If you have clearly identified a preference for one or two interest areas you should find it easier to make career decisions because you have well-formed preferences about the sort of work that will interest you.

On the other hand, if your interests seem to be in several different areas, it may be that you will need to do some research about jobs and how they differ before you can tell where your specific interests lie.

It may be that you have been put off a certain area of work by a bad experience (e.g. an unsympathetic boss) or from trying to do a job without the necessary training.

You also need to find out whether your interests seem to be pointing you towards one single part of the map or to several different parts. You can find this out by going back to the diagram which shows how the six interest areas relate to the

two axes, **People/Things** and **Data/Ideas**. Are the two interest areas for which you have the strongest preference alongside each other in this diagram?

If they are, this suggests that the sort of jobs that are available in this area will offer you opportunities for interesting work.

If you find that your interests are in areas that are not alongside each other in the diagram, this suggests that you may have to look more widely at jobs from the two or more areas that might interest you. However, many jobs can satisfy more than one area of interest. Frequently, you can identify a type of work that satisfies your strongest area of interest but choose to pursue it in an environment or work setting that will satisfy your other area of interest. In this way you could work alongside people doing different jobs but who have similar interests. For example, working as a secretary in an advertising agency or a social services department is likely to offer very different kinds of work colleagues.

Are you where you want to be?

By completing the two exercises you should have identified the sort of activities you would enjoy in your work. Now ask yourself whether your present job (or alternatively your last job) contained these sort of activities.

Exercise 4: my current or recent work activities

The easiest way to do this is to repeat Exercise 2 'Your work interests', only this time ask yourself as you rate each activity: 'Does my current (last) job involve ...?'

Circle one number alongside each activity using the new scale from 1 – not at all to 5 – a very great deal.

Now add up the score for each set of items (maximum score for each area is 25). Then list in your notebook the six types of activity in rank order from rank 1 for the highest-scoring set of items to rank 6 for the lowest. This is the interest profile for your current (or most recent) job.

How does this job compare with your preferences? Does it offer you the sort of activities that you enjoy? Compare the three highest-scoring activity areas from the two exercises:

	Exercise 2	Exercise 4
	My interests	*My current/last job*
Highest		
Second		
Third		

If it does, this does not necessarily mean that you should not be reviewing your career plans or even looking for a job change, but it should reassure you that you are already in the right area of the map of work interests. This is likely to help in your planning, because you are more likely to know about jobs similar to your present one.

If your current or last job does not offer activities that are important to you or offers only some of them, this is one important reason for reviewing your career plans.

27

Summary

We have spent today:

- learning about the key dimensions of work interests
- reviewing the work activities that you enjoy
- considering the extent to which your current or last job satisfies your work interests

This is important because doing work we find interesting is likely to be enjoyable in the long-term. It is also likely to bring out the best in us because we will be motivated to do it and will make the extra effort to do it well.

By identifying the sort of activities you enjoy, you have now identified where you want to be on the map of work interests in an ideal world. Also, by reviewing your current or last job you have an idea about where you are starting out from. You should now be in a strong position to review your skills, knowledge and experience to see whether you are equipped for the sort of work opportunities that are available there.

Later in the week, we will put all that you have learnt about yourself – values, interests and skills – together with what you have learnt about the world of work to make some choices about your career options and formulate an action plan.

SUNDAY
MONDAY
TUESDAY
WEDNESDAY
THURSDAY
FRIDAY
SATURDAY

Questions

Questions to check your understanding

1. We want to understand what interests us to find out:
   a) What we are good at ❏
   b) What we enjoy ❏
   c) What we have learnt ❏
   d) Where there are job opportunities ❏

2. The best way to find out about our interests is to:
   a) Review the sort of work we have done in the past ❏
   b) Decide whether we enjoy our current job ❏
   c) Review our skills, knowledge and experience ❏
   d) Systematically assess how much different work activities interest us ❏

3. Understanding what we enjoy helps us:
   a) Identify jobs that might interest us ❏
   b) Identify what we are good at ❏
   c) Know whether we have the skills we need ❏
   d) Decide how satisfied we are at work ❏

Questions to capture your reflections

1. In which three of the six areas of work interests do you score highest?
2. The kind of work I would enjoy would involve...
3. How would you explain to a job interviewer why you are interested in this kind of work?
4. How well did your current/last job match your work interests? What were its most and least interesting aspects for you?
5. In what ways have your interests changed over the last few years?
6. What reasons may have put you off pursuing potentially interesting areas of work in the past?
7. What is the most important thing you have learned today about your work interests?

TUESDAY

What are you good at?

Having thought about where your job interests lie, you now need to move on to think about your skills, knowledge and experience. This means both being aware of why you need to assess yourself as well as having some techniques for carrying out this assessment. This requires:

- understanding the need for self-assessment
- using exercises to review your skills and experience
- deciding whether you like what you are good at

In thinking about what you are good at, it is important not just to think about what you do in your present job but also to include what you have done in previous jobs and outside of paid work. Sometimes the skills, knowledge and experiences you have gained outside of paid employment could be applied at work and so it is important to consider them as well, especially if you have not been in paid work for a while, or are looking for your first job.

Understanding the need for self-assessment

If we were concerned with selecting someone for a job, we would want to assure ourselves that they were capable of doing it. What sort of evidence of their ability to do the job – their 'competence' – would we consider relevant?

Almost certainly we would want evidence of the kind of work they had done previously. This would help us determine whether they were likely to have the skills, knowledge and experience required for the job. We might also want to know about their educational qualifications. Educational qualifications give a broad indication of overall level of ability and show whether someone has the specific skills and knowledge required for certain types of work. Having the right qualifications is essential to be considered for many types of work. We would also want to check whether they have certain key skills, e.g. basic computer skills, communication skills, numeracy.

The weight given to each of these components will vary considerably for different sorts of jobs. Qualifications are important for technical and professional jobs; they may be less important for non-technical and managerial jobs, where skills and experience are the main indicators of suitability. Selectors will also give more weight to recent work history than to qualifications that were gained many years ago.

It is just the same for you when trying to determine whether you are qualified to do certain sorts of job. You have to review your skills, knowledge and experience, as well as your educational qualifications, to work out what sort of jobs you may be capable of doing.

And finally, it is worth remembering that we are much more likely to enjoy working in a job where we will perform well rather than in one where we will struggle to do the work involved.

Assessing skills and experience

Of course, you are not yet at the stage of being selected for a job. Rather, you are trying to work out what jobs you might be able to do. *How are you going to do this?*

Answer 1: using your expert knowledge

In some circumstances, selectors go out and measure the performance of people who are currently doing the same job elsewhere, to build up an objective picture of the skills required for the job. In this process they may use tests, measures of work output (e.g. production figures), ratings of performance from managers and so on. Frequently, however, it is not possible to collect this kind of objective information. Selectors therefore have to make their own judgements about the skills, knowledge and experience that are required for the job. It is generally assumed that selectors are able to do this because of their expert knowledge.

This is what you are going to do today. You will use your expert knowledge of yourself to review the skills, knowledge and experience you have acquired throughout your life.

The strength of this approach is that no one should know you better than you know yourself. However, for this approach to be successful requires strict honesty in assessment. After all, someone who is not honest in self-assessment fools no one but themselves.

Answer 2: using exercises

The remainder of today is going to be spent in completing and interpreting two exercises. These exercises are designed to help you review your skills, knowledge and experience. The first exercise aims to give you an opportunity to make an overall assessment of your skill level, while the second one aims to generate a more detailed list of the skills, knowledge and experience you have acquired.

Of course, two short self-completion exercises do not constitute a thorough assessment of your skills; the aim here is to get started on the self-assessment process and to enable you to see in what broad areas you feel you have skills. Several of the books and websites in the Guide to resources at the back of the book contain additional exercises that can be used to give a more detailed assessment.

Exercise 5: identifying your areas of strength
This exercise asks you to judge how your skills compare with those of other people. Think about your skills in relation to the four compass points of our work map:

People: work skills involved in working with people might include managing and organizing people, persuading and negotiating with people, supporting and giving help to people, teaching, entertaining or understanding other people.

Things: work skills involved in making or constructing things might include the manual skills in using tools and working with machinery, the ability to understand how things work, having good hand-eye coordination.

Data: work skills involved in handling information might include interpreting a graph, working with figures on a computer, deciding how best to present and communicate information.

Ideas: work skills associated with being creative might include designing or adapting things, improvising, being innovative, having an interest in ideas and how to develop them, experimenting and investigating.

First of all, rate yourself in comparison to people in general. Compared to other people, how good are you at working with people, things, data and ideas? Circle the appropriate phrase in each case:

People
Excellent   Very good   Quite good   Not very good   No good at all

Things
Excellent   Very good   Quite good   Not very good   No good at all

Data
Excellent   Very good   Quite good   Not very good   No good at all

Ideas
Excellent   Very good   Quite good   Not very good   No good at all

How do you rate yourself? Have you given yourself a similar rating for each of the four skill areas, or do you think that you have a higher level of skills in some areas than in others?

Next, try rating yourself again, only this time making your comparisons in terms of people doing the sort of jobs in which you are interested.

These are your self-ratings of your skills. They are a measure of how you see your skills in relation to those of other people.

How accurate are these judgements? One way of testing this is to get someone else who knows you well to rate you in these four skill areas. Some of us are modest and tend to underestimate our skills, while others of us are more generous in the way we rate ourselves. Getting a second opinion is one way of finding out whether our perceptions match those of others (friends, work colleagues, or family).

You may find it helpful to summarize the results from these ratings by you and others in your notebook using the table below as a template:

How do I compare?

	People	Things	Data	Ideas
People in general				
People doing this type of work				
How do others rate me?				

The next exercise aims to review in more detail your skills, knowledge and experience.

Exercise 6: reviewing your skills, knowledge and experience
The only way to do this is to review things you have already done and to think hard about what they involved. This exercise uses the same four headings as in Exercise 5; this makes it easy to look at the results of both exercises together. This exercise needs to be done in several stages.

The first step is to think of things you have done: for example, your current job (if you have one), a previous job that you liked, a previous job that you disliked, something you have carried out (a serious hobby or outside interest), a role you have experienced (parent, student). There is no limit to the number that can be listed. Try to list two or three to start with.

Next, you need to identify the activities that were involved in the jobs or roles that you have listed. Write some of the activities that make up each job or role on a new page of your notebook. Looking at these activities will help you identify the skills, knowledge and experience you have used.

Now, using a fresh page, write at the top the name of the job or role you are reviewing, then write down the left-hand side the three headings, **Skills**, **Knowledge**, **Experience**, equally spaced down the sheet. You will need a new page like this for each job/role you examine.

Now try to list the *skills* that are associated with each of the activities that you have listed. Include both general skills and more specific ones. You will need to ask yourself these kinds of questions for each job or role:

- Did you work with people? If so, in what way? Persuading them or selling something to them? Teaching or training them? Communicating with them? Was leadership involved?
- Did you work with things? What sort of things? Machines or tools? Working out how to make something? Were physical skills, like hand-eye coordination, important?
- Did you work with data? How? Did you have to organize or administer it? Were you collating information or figures? Were financial skills involved? Was attention to detail important? Were particular computer skills used?

- Did you work with ideas? Were you creating something? Did this include designing something? Researching or finding out about it? How did you plan this work?

Next list the *knowledge* that you used when carrying out the activities in each job or role.

- Did you have relevant educational, academic or professional qualifications? What knowledge did you acquire from doing this job/role?

Third, list the *experience* you gained from doing this job/role.

- Did you work as part of a team or on your own? What special experience do you associate with this job/role? Was there anything you really disliked about it?

Finally, it is also important to think whether any of your personal qualities were relevant to how you performed in this job/role. These might have been a help – 'my persistence is what got the job done' – or a hindrance – 'I couldn't see the point of what I was supposed to be doing.' Sometimes this is an indication of work matching or not matching with your work values.

Before the final part of the exercise, make several copies of the chart below with three rows headed *Skills*, *Knowledge*, *Experience* and four columns headed *People*, *Things*, *Data*, *Ideas*. One copy can then be completed for each of your roles.

	People	Things	Data	Ideas
Skills				
Knowledge				
Experience				

Having written your entries under the three headings *Skills, Knowledge, Experience* you can then go on to classify them under the four headings *People, Things, Data, Ideas*.

Once you have completed one job or role, repeat the process for the second one, and so on.

Putting it all together

The final stage of the exercise is to go through all your completed forms and look at what you have listed. For each entry, whether it is under skills, knowledge or experience, you must decide whether you were good at it.

Now make another copy of the master form and summarize, in the appropriate box, the things that you are good at.

Making sense of all this

You should now be in a position to review what you have learned about yourself.

First of all, can you see any pattern in skills, knowledge and experience you have acquired? Have some things come up several times? Are they in the same categories?

Are you good at them? Is there a pattern in the things you are good at? What are you *really* good at?

Looking at this list of things you are good at, it is now appropriate to ask yourself: Do you like doing these things? Of these, which ones are really important to you? Which ones would you like to do more?

Don't forget to make a note of the personal qualities that you offer.

Linking skills to jobs

As well as the very detailed profile you have now built up about yourself, you also need to be able to summarize where you think you should be located on the map of work types.

Look at the 'wheel' diagram. Colour, tick or mark in some other way the sectors of the wheel where you now know you have skills, knowledge or experience. The areas can be related to the results from Monday's exercises on work interests.

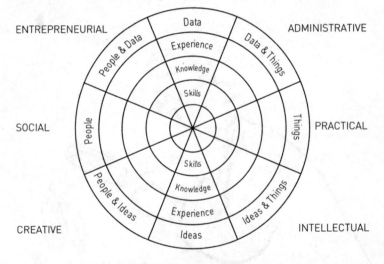

Check back with Exercise 5. Do the results of the two exercises agree? Having completed Exercise 6, do you want to change the way you have rated yourself on Exercise 5?

Are your skills in:

● adjacent sectors?
● opposite sectors?
● more than half the sectors?

Are your areas of strength the same as your areas of interest?

Learning for the future

As work will continue to change, one key skill for everyone is being prepared to learn new skills. Nowadays, nearly every job requires some computer skills, for example. Employers are increasingly interested in our willingness to learn and try out new things. Our attitude to learning can be just as important as our existing skills, knowledge and experience.

Summary

We have spent Tuesday reviewing what you are good at. We have set out to:

- understand why you need to do this
- review your skills, knowledge and experience
- see how they relate to the four areas of data, ideas, people and things
- map out these areas
- show why learning new skills is important.

Understanding our strengths, as well as having some insight into our weaknesses, is crucial if we are to be successful in the labour market. We want to play to our strengths as these are what will make us attractive to potential employers. This will enable us to make sure that we concentrate our efforts where we are most likely to be successful. One goal of today has been to identify what our areas of strength are and we will use this information when we develop our career plan on Friday.

You will want to use this information to highlight some of your particular skills in your CV. Both you and potential employers will want to build on your strengths. This is something we will consider in more detail on Saturday.

SUNDAY

MONDAY

TUESDAY

WEDNESDAY

THURSDAY

FRIDAY

SATURDAY

Questions

Questions to check your understanding

1. We need to know what we are good at:
a) To decide whether we are capable of doing different jobs ☐
b) To see what interests us ☐
c) Because it is difficult to find work ☐
d) To discover what we have learnt ☐

2. Getting someone else to rate my skills:
a) Is good for my self-esteem ☐
b) Helps me know whether my perceptions are accurate ☐
c) Tells me that I am not as clever as I thought ☐
d) Identifies possible work areas ☐

3. Learning new skills is important because:
a) Employers will want me to learn things ☐
b) I don't have many skills ☐
c) I am finding it difficult to get a job ☐
d) Computers have changed everything ☐

Questions to capture your reflections

1. What are your two key strengths out of the four 'compass points' you looked at?
2. What personal qualities do you bring to your work and how would other people see these?
3. Other people say that I am good at...
4. How similar are your areas of strength to your work interests? In what ways?
5. Are there skills, knowledge and experience you have gained outside work, which you could use at work? If so, what are they?
6. Which three aspects of your skills, knowledge and experience might be especially relevant to an employer in some of your interest areas? For each one, can you describe a real situation in which you have applied that ability?
7. A work-related skill that I have recently acquired is...

WEDNESDAY

Identifying your career options

You have started the career planning process by learning about yourself: examining your own values, interests, skills, knowledge and experience. Now it is time to turn to the second major building block of the career planning framework: learning about jobs. We will spread this task over the next two days. Today, we start by thinking as widely as possible about career options.

You may find that some career options which look exciting turn out to be less attractive or less achievable when you know more about them. You may need to go through the process of generating options and researching them several times before you move on to make a career action plan.

Today we will examine:

- what is happening to jobs and careers
- what kinds of jobs there are
- your own career options

In identifying our options, we need to understand what is happening to jobs and employment in our country or region and also in the sectors and occupations which interest us. You should try to think widely at this stage about your possible future directions. There will be time tomorrow to check them out more carefully in terms of how realistic and achievable they may be.

What is happening to jobs and careers?

When we think about our own career options, it is important to be aware of general trends in the world of work. The job market is always changing, both short term and longer term.

The economy

The state of the economy clearly affects our job options. In a recession, opportunities are likely to be in short supply. In a period of rapid economic growth, there are more job vacancies. These are not caused just by new jobs but also by people moving more freely from job to job. It will be easier at such times to re-enter the labour market or make radical career moves.

Also, the job market varies between sectors of the economy, parts of the country and countries across the world. Some types of employer can be recruiting while others are reducing numbers.

When you are trying to get into a particular type of work in a period of recession or slow growth you may need to enter organizations at a lower level than you wish, simply to get a foot in the door. Often, once employed, you may then find it easier to work your way into a job which is closer to what you had hoped for.

The media report economic information, often mentioning aspects of the job market, sometimes on a geographical basis. We should use this knowledge to decide the tactics of our job moves. Given the turbulence of economic conditions, however, we should not let short-term economic changes dominate our longer-term career strategy.

Longer-term changes in jobs and careers

More important to your longer-term career options are underlying shifts in the employment structure and in employer behaviour. These vary in detail by country, region and sector, but some broad shifts occurred in most Western nations in the late 20th century:

- a reduction of employment in so-called 'primary' sectors, e.g. agriculture, fishing, mining
- relatively fewer jobs in manufacturing industry
- relatively more jobs in the service sectors, e.g. retailing, financial services, health and personal services
- an increase in the relative importance of employment in smaller organizations and of self-employment
- the 'contracting out' of some work from larger organizations (e.g. in security, catering, cleaning) to smaller organizations or the self-employed
- the movement of some kinds of work (e.g. call centre operations) to countries where they could be delivered more cheaply and, for example in R&D, to where highly skilled people are easily available but at lower salaries
- a growth in temporary and part-time employment
- a growth in high-skill, professional and 'knowledge' jobs and a rising proportion of the population with degree-level qualifications.

These changes have resulted in significant levels of general unemployment, coexisting with shortages of people with particular skills.

However, some long-term trends appeared to have slowed down by the turn of the century. For example, in the UK the proportion of people who are self-employed or who work part-time seems to have levelled out and the number of portfolio workers remains very small overall (less than 5%). However, these ways of working are common in some occupations, such as the creative industries. A small but growing number of people work from home, at least part of the time.

Low-skilled jobs have not disappeared as quickly as economists thought they would, leading to what some call 'hour glass' labour markets in developed economies with an increasing proportion of professional and managerial jobs, but also a lot of fairly low skilled and low paid jobs, mostly in services (e.g. cleaning, catering, hospitality, retail, health and social care).

These shifts in employment, plus alterations to the way large organizations operate, have also changed careers:

- A 'job for life' is not a realistic expectation. We should expect several major changes in occupation during our working lives, and many more in job or employer.
- Large organizations expect their employees to manage their own career moves and skill development.
- Many labour markets have become very specialized with employers looking for specific skills and experience as well as strong generic skills.
- We may, at some times in our lives, need to significantly retrain and gain new qualifications.
- In some sectors (e.g. politics and the media), periods of unpaid work or 'internships' are becoming the norm for those trying to enter work.
- Many people will be retiring later, some because they wish to work longer and others because rapidly changing pension arrangements make it a financial necessity.
- Technology has affected the recruitment process with a growth in on-line job applications and initial tests. Only after success in these first stages will you get the chance to meet a potential employer face-to-face.

More information on jobs is now within our reach, but these changes to employment have made labour markets more complex for individuals to navigate successfully.

Managing our own career

To manage our own careers in these complex, competitive and ever-shifting labour markets, we need to develop:

- flexibility and adaptability
- ability to learn new skills, especially higher-level, interpersonal and technological skills
- willingness and ability to manage our own careers
- ability to develop and use personal networks to get work
- ability to see and understand trends in the labour market.

Kinds of jobs

Most of us are restricted in our career planning by our very limited knowledge of the jobs that exist. We know about the jobs that our parents, friends and teachers do or tell us about. There are many jobs we never consider because we do not know about them. So how do we start thinking about jobs?

A useful starting point is to take the same concepts we used on Monday to map work interests. We can look at jobs in terms of whether they predominantly involve working with people, things, data or ideas.

We used six headings to think about activities and interests, and the same categories can be used again to think about broad 'families' of jobs, as follows:

- 'entrepreneurial': business and management jobs
- 'administrative' or organizational jobs
- 'practical' or technical jobs ◁
- 'intellectual': scientific and research jobs ⊢
- 'creative' and artistic jobs ↖
- 'social' and personal services jobs

Within each family there are jobs at various levels, in various sectors and with a range of specific content. A few illustrations might help your imagination to get going. While reading this section, keep a note of any jobs which seem worth exploring.

SUNDAY MONDAY TUESDAY WEDNESDAY THURSDAY FRIDAY SATURDAY

Entrepreneurial jobs include: jobs in business and management, marketing and selling such as telephone sales, marketing manager, retail manager, shop assistant, buyer, personnel manager, estate agent.

Administrative and organizational jobs include: clerical, secretarial and administrative jobs, jobs in finance, actuaries, tax consultants, management accountants.

Practical and technical jobs include: a vast number of jobs working with different materials and technologies and at a wide range of levels, from labourers to nuclear engineers, such as jobs in construction (e.g. building trades, surveyor), in manufacturing (e.g. operators, technicians), in transport, engineering, leisure (e.g. domestic staff, chef), agriculture and horticulture (e.g. gardener, tree surgeon, vet).

Intellectual jobs include: jobs in research, science, medicine and social sciences, such as laboratory technician, geologist, statistician, radiographer, nutritionist, surgeon, economist, maths teacher.

Creative and artistic jobs include: music, dance, theatre and the visual arts, director, producer, journalist, professional sport, advertising, fashion work, architecture and design, photography.

Social and personal service jobs include: playleader, teacher, lecturer, social worker, counsellor, hotel receptionist, air steward/stewardess, beauty therapist, prison officer.

Of course, there are jobs which combine elements of more than one family. For example, technical jobs in the arts (e.g.

theatrical electrician, sound technician) combine creative with technical skills. Many jobs in health and the law (e.g. nurse, barrister) combine personal and scientific or research skills.

Identifying career options

Now it is time to generate your own list of career options. It is important that at this stage you think as widely – even wildly – as possible. Even if you eventually decide to stick with the same job, or a very similar one, such exploration will reassure you that you *are* in the right line of work, at least for now.

Types of career options

You can think about your career options in terms of how far away they are from what you are doing now, or did most recently when you were last at work.

Types of options might include:

- changing the content of your current job
- moving to a job for which you have the skills
- moving to a job requiring some further training or job experiences
- making a major career change into a new area of work, often requiring new qualifications
- other changes, e.g. taking a break from work, voluntary work, going back into full-time education, becoming self-employed.

Generating a list of options

There is no single best way to approach this task. You may already have several options in mind; or you may be starting with a blank sheet of paper.

Here are some of the starting points you could use in listing your own career options. Jot down any ideas that come to mind as you think in your notebook.

- Do some of the 'families' of jobs described above excite you or contain jobs you have always wanted to do? Look back at the work you have done on your values (Exercise 1), interests

(Exercises 2, 3 and 4) and skills (Exercises 5 and 6) to identify at least some job families which are likely to suit you.

- If job families seem too general, some more detailed careers material contains lists of jobs within each of these families (see Guide to resources at the end of this book).
- Think about the different types of career option listed above.
- Fantasize about the perfect job. What would a perfect working day consist of? What would you be doing, and in what surroundings?
- Talk to family, friends and colleagues.
- Look at job advertisements in newspapers and journals.
- If you are in employment, look afresh at your current job and consider whether it would meet your needs if you could change it in some way.
- Think too about jobs elsewhere in your current organization – not just promotions but also jobs in other locations, in other departments or units, and in other functions or occupations.

LIFE BY THE POOL ISN'T AS IDYLLIC AS I'D HOPED

For each of your options, try to think about where your desired activities or jobs might exist. Identify:

- possible sectors, types of employer or particular organizations
- whether any options involve things other than conventional paid employment, e.g. voluntary work, self-employment, full-time study, working from home.

It is important to think too about some of the implications of each option, such as money, working time, geographical location or the need to study.

Listing and summarizing your career options

This part of our process should have helped you to generate several career options. You should summarize these before moving on.

Exercise 7: summarizing career options

First write a simple list of each of the career options so far identified. Remember you can always come back to this list and add more options later if you choose.

For example, someone re-entering paid employment after several years caring for their young children might be considering:

- going back to teaching
- becoming an educational psychologist
- some form of self-employment – perhaps writing.

A young graduate accountant might include:

- gaining faster promotion to partner
- moving to a larger firm
- finance work in another sector, perhaps retail
- doing something quite different once qualified: taking a management course, travelling.

Now you need to complete a summary sheet for each of your options, recording the most important things about it. A sample format for this summary is shown below and you might like to use it in your notebook.

In looking at each career option, it is important to be honest with yourself about its likely pros and cons. Think about how they might affect your partner or family as well as yourself. Are there trade-offs between the contract of employment (e.g. money, location) and how attracted you are by the work itself? What about the kinds of people you might be working with and the likely workplace culture?

Pay attention to how you *feel* about each option as well as your more objective assessment of it, before you go on to research it further.

Career Option Summary

Name/title for this option

Type of option *(circle one or add your own)*:
- changing content of your current job
- moving to a job for which you have the skills
- moving to a job requiring training/experience
- a major career change
- other (e.g. changing pattern of work)

Job family, job activities or occupations involved *(including possible jobs if known)*:

Possible employer or job context *(particular employers or types of employer, voluntary work, self-employed, full-time education, etc.)*:

Implications of this option *(finance, patterns of work, location, requirements for education or training)*:

Pros and cons of this option:

Summary

We have spent Wednesday considering:

- what is happening to jobs and careers
- what types of jobs there are
- your own career options

Labour markets are always changing. Some changes are caused by economic fluctuations but other trends occur over a longer period of time. Many economies, including that of the UK, now need more people with high level skills and qualifications and many highly skilled jobs have become very specialized. But low-skilled jobs have also persisted. Flexible working has been growing but there is no sign that conventional paid employment is being swept away on a tide of portfolio working or self-employment. Employment in small businesses is an important part of the economy and when we think about careers we should not just think about large employers.

Even in good times these trends add up to more complex and challenging labour markets to navigate. So we need better skills to manage our own careers effectively.

SUNDAY

MONDAY

TUESDAY

WEDNESDAY

THURSDAY

FRIDAY

SATURDAY

We can use the same simple framework for both job interests (as you did on Monday) and job options as we have done today.

Today you have used your previous work on interests and your understanding of the labour market to identify some of your career options. These may involve changing job or even a much more radical change in career. But options can also include changing the content of your current job or your work pattern.

Your work tomorrow will be to find out more about what each of your options would actually involve.

Questions

Questions to check your understanding

1. A frequent problem in career planning is that:
a) There are many jobs which might suit us well, but we don't know about them ❑
b) We consider too wide a range of options ❑
c) We are too slow to make a final choice ❑
d) There is little information available ❑

2. Which of these statements reflects labour market trends in most developed economies?
a) Low-skill jobs have nearly disappeared ❑
b) The proportion of jobs which are professional and managerial has grown ❑
c) Most people work in manufacturing ❑
d) Most people are now 'portfolio' workers ❑

3. When the economy is doing well, it is a good time to:
a) Sit tight ❑
b) Make a significant career move ❑
c) Stop planning ❑
d) Wait for a new employer to approach you ❑

Questions to capture your reflections

1. The section on labour market trends made me more aware of...
2. When I thought about my perfect job or perfect working day, I realized...
3. The main career options I have identified so far are: ...
4. Are your options in the job families which you have identified as interesting to you?
5. Which options, if any, might require significant further training or qualifications?
6. Which options, if any, could be achieved by changing some aspects of your current job or moving to another job in the same organization?
7. Which options appeal most strongly to you at this stage and why?

THURSDAY

Collecting information

Now you have drawn up a list of career options, how do you move towards an action plan? It is tempting to move straight to choosing an option or applying for jobs. It is also unwise. We usually need to know a good deal more about each of our options before we are in a position to make judgements about them. This phase of 'active job research' makes all the difference between good career decisions and poor ones.

Today you need to turn from a dreamer into a detective. Your elusive quarry will be the real job. You need to know what it would feel like to do the kinds of work you are considering. But it is also important to understand how people get into this kind of work as you may need to invest in gaining particular qualifications and/or work experience before you would be considered a credible job candidate.

Only when you have a good understanding of what each of your options really involves can you make a wise choice.

We will be examining:

- your information needs
- career paths
- sources of information on careers and jobs
- using information interviews

Your information needs

There are three main sets of questions you need to answer when you are researching jobs:

What would this option really be like?

- In what environment would you be working?
- What would you be doing?
- What are the likely conditions of employment?

What would you need?

- What skills are required?
- What knowledge or qualifications are required?
- What previous experience is required?

Will there be opportunities available?

We discuss each of these areas in more detail below and later in the chapter we will look at how you find the answers. Once you have the answers to these questions, then you can compare them with your own values, interests, skills, knowledge and experience to decide which options will suit you best.

The same questions can be applied to career options which are not just job moves. For example, if you are considering self-employment you can ask yourself what that change will really mean for you, what skills you will need, and whether you can create a realistic opportunity for yourself.

Exercise 8: career option research
This exercise goes a step further from the brief description of each option you generated yesterday. The blank form shows some headings you might use for each option to structure the information you collect.

The notes on the headings suggest some of the specific things you should be finding out.

You may like to make up a page like this in your notebook for each of your main options. It will make a useful summary you can use in this exercise, but also keep coming back to as you find out more.

Career Option Research
Name/title of career option

What would this option really be like?
Work environment *(employers, values, environment)*:

Job content *(role, level, responsibilities, activities)*:

Conditions of employment *(e.g. pay, hours)*:

Requirements for this option
Skills/knowledge:

Qualifications:

Previous job/career experience:

Likely levels of opportunity

SUNDAY
MONDAY
TUESDAY
WEDNESDAY
THURSDAY
FRIDAY
SATURDAY

Work environment matters as well as the content of a job, and choosing an environment which is compatible with your work values can be crucial. From a practical point of view, you need to find out who your likely employers might be. You also need to know with what sorts of people you will be working: your colleagues and how much you might interact with them, and also the kind of manager you might have and the client or customer contact which is likely. The physical environment in which we work is also important, including where work could be located. When looking at particular sectors or employers, the culture of the organization is important. By culture we mean how things are done, e.g. how formally or informally people behave. Later on, these items will tell you to what extent each option is compatible with your personal values.

Job content is of paramount importance, including:

- What is this job there to do (job role) and how does it fit into the organization?
- If the job exists at more than one level, into which job levels might you fit, perhaps in both the short and the longer term?
- What are job holders' responsibilities?
- What would a typical working day involve?
- How predictable is the work? Is it stressful? How much freedom and autonomy do job holders have?

Conditions of employment need to cover the financial and domestic implications of each option, e.g. pay, benefits, pensions, costs of education courses, working hours and patterns (real not just contractual), travelling or working away, possible relocation.

Work environment, job content and conditions of employment tell you what each career option would really feel like. They apply just as much to full-time education or self-employment as to conventional jobs. For example, many people like working from home some of the time but might get lonely doing it all the time if there is no reason to visit customers, suppliers or colleagues.

Skills and knowledge requirements tell us:

- what we have to be able to do
- what we have to know about.

You will be using this information later to assess your suitability for each option, and to present your curriculum vitae (CV) in the best way.

It is often possible to extrapolate from job activities to the skills and knowledge required. For example, the school-teacher thinking of writing educational materials would have to get ideas accepted by publishers, research, design and write. Skills required would include imagination, persuasion, negotiation, research, writing at the right level, computer skills, project and time management. Knowledge of the market would also be critical and the ability to learn how to run a small business.

Formal **qualifications** are used by employers as another 'filter' for applicants. For some jobs, including many professions, they are a statutory requirement. Many career paths require qualifications to get beyond a certain level so you need to find out which qualifications are necessary or preferred for your chosen option.

When employers are short of good applicants they tend to be somewhat flexible about qualification requirements. When lots of good people are competing for few vacancies, employers often sift for higher level or more specific qualifications as part of the short-listing process.

There is a rough association between job level and level of qualifications required:

● no formal qualifications: mainly unskilled and semi-skilled jobs
● general qualifications from school: many clerical and craft jobs, often followed by specific vocational training
● higher-level qualifications: many jobs require good school-leaving qualifications plus specific vocational training, but not a degree
● degree or professional qualifications: most specialist jobs and, increasingly, management

Skills and knowledge are what we need to do a job, but employers often use what we have done before – our **previous job/career experience** – as an indicator of these. In many walks of life there are jobs which are difficult to enter without having done some of the activities before, often at a more junior level. Sometimes you may be able to convince an employer to take a chance on you, even if you do not have the usual background experience. However, you still should arm yourself with the knowledge of what previous experience is normally expected. You need to know:

● the types of jobs and job levels at which you can enter your desired organization or occupation
● the subsequent sequences of job experience – career paths – which are most often followed
● the range of experience expected for your desired job.

The skills, knowledge, qualifications and experience which an employer is looking for translate into the things the recruitment and selection process will look for, called the *selection criteria*. Career and job information (e.g. job advertisements) often tell you the selection criteria. You need to look at these most carefully when writing your job application or CV or preparing for an interview. Look out also for how the organization describes its culture – this information on how the organization likes people to behave at work can also be important in selection.

Mapping career paths

If you find the career paths hard to think about for any of your particular options, it can help to try and map them. This is especially helpful for options which involve quite a few job or training steps between where you are now and where you want to be. Career path maps can be drawn for an occupation (e.g. entering educational psychology as a new career) or for more specific options within a given employer (e.g. the young accountant wanting to make his/her way to a partnership).

Exercise 9: drawing a career path map
Try drawing a map for some of your options which involve several job steps. Show boxes for relevant types of job

experience. Put more junior jobs lower down on the page and more senior jobs higher up, with job levels in different work areas roughly lined up across the page. Arrows show career moves between boxes, which may involve a change in:

- level or job role
- department, unit or location
- function (e.g. production, personnel, sales)
- employer.

If you are trying to enter an organization, you should mark the jobs where external recruitment occurs.

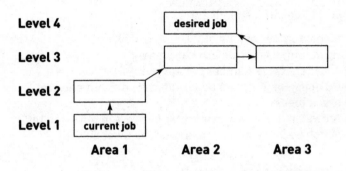

The typical career map shown here illustrates a career option involving a desired job type three levels above the current job (these may be from trainee, to qualified, to supervisor, to manager). It also shows moving to an area of work (Area 2) different from the current one (Area 1). To achieve this, it may be necessary to gain experience in a third area (Area 3).

These areas of work may be functions (e.g. production, finance, sales), different parts of the same function, different units (factory, head office) or different locations (e.g. a small-town bank, a large city branch, an international operation). They might also represent different employers. Often the map will show more than one possible route to where you want to get.

You can use these maps to identify more clearly short- and longer-term job goals.

Likely levels of opportunity

We have already discussed changing employment patterns and the labour shortages and surpluses they bring. It is important to be aware which career options will offer plenty of opportunity and which will be very competitive.

High levels of opportunity are found in:

- new or rapidly growing areas of activity or new technologies
- occupations for which few people have been training, and where shortages may develop
- occupations from which many people are about to retire, and where replacements will be needed.

Your job research should ask:

- Is the number of jobs growing or shrinking?
- How many vacancies exist at present?
- Are there large numbers of applicants?
- Do opportunities vary geographically or from one employer to another?
- Are you likely to face particular barriers in pursuing this option because of age, gender, race, disability, etc.?

Information sources

Your information needs will be quite wide ranging, as we have seen above, but there are many sources of job information. The process itself can be fun and interesting. Your main access to job information will be through:

- people you know – your personal network
- external information sources
- information within your own organization
- people doing the job – through information interviews.

People you know (colleagues, friends and family) may know about the job you have in mind, or have a friend who does. They may know about the organization you are considering, or the college course you might take. It is always better to talk to someone who has had real contact with a job, rather than just listen to general opinions. If you know 100 people, and they each know 100 people, that gives you 10 000 people to ask – assuming you all have different friends!

Social networking sites can be useful for tracking down people you know, but have not seen for a while, who you think may have done the kind of job or course you are interested in. Many educational institutions have alumni websites or networks which put you in touch with people who studied at your school, college or university. Email makes it easier to approach people – both those you know personally and others you find via your networks – and to see if they might be willing to give you some information.

External information sources include:

- brochures and reports from potential employers
- press and journals: job advertisements and articles on job and career trends
- reference books, career directories and reference material, available in public libraries
- careers services and educational institutions
- recruitment agencies
- industry and professional bodies: these often produce the most comprehensive and reliable information both on careers and on qualifications required, and should keep it up-to-date
- trade unions and employee organizations.

SUNDAY
MONDAY
TUESDAY
WEDNESDAY
THURSDAY
FRIDAY
SATURDAY

Much of this information is now accessible via simple internet searches and published on organization' websites.

Information within your own organization can be very useful if you are currently employed and considering career options within the same organization. However, make careful judgements about whom you talk to and when. Choose people who will keep a confidence if asked to.

There are many other internal information sources:

- Business information (e.g. annual reports, newsletters, business plans or objectives) is usually freely available.
- Job vacancies are often put on notice-boards or intranet sites.
- The HR function usually holds information on jobs, e.g. recruitment literature, training schemes, organization charts, job descriptions, skill and qualification requirements.
- Some employers have special libraries or on-line systems containing information on careers and training.
- Successful people in the job area you have in mind provide useful clues as to what career paths are valued, and what skills are required.
- Senior people, including your own boss, are often happy to advise or take a 'mentoring' role. Try and approach people who you think will support you. Use your own friends and informal networks to find out who might be best to speak to.

Career information can often be inaccurate, out of date or biased. When using the internet and also when asking individuals for job or training information, you always need to think carefully about who the information is coming from and therefore how to assess its quality and objectivity. Consider, for example, whether:

- your information source is likely to have valid data or relevant experience to base any opinion on
- such data and opinion are sufficiently up-to-date to be relevant and apply to your personal situation, life-stage, country or locality
- they may have any reason to influence you to make a particular decision. For example, colleges on the whole

want students and so tend to encourage applicants. Those working in a field may be either very enthusiastic or quite tired of it.

Once you have done some preparatory research it can be extremely valuable to talk to someone who actually does the job you have in mind. We call this an *information interview*.

Information interviews do not just help your research. They also give you a chance to meet people who might be willing to help you later on, or to recommend other useful contacts.

If you are approaching someone you do not know well for an information interview, think about how you should approach them so as to appear polite and considerate in your request. This is especially important if approaching someone in another country or from another culture.

When conducting an information interview:

- explain that the purpose of the interview is to help you find out more about a type of job in which you are interested
- prepare in advance what you are going to say and ask
- arrive on time and take the same care with your personal appearance (if meeting face-to-face) as you would for a job interview
- take good notes
- keep it short and check at the start how long they are expecting to talk to you for

- be pleasant and not too pushy, but take a CV with you just in case (e.g. see 'Putting something down in writing' in Saturday)
- send a thank-you letter or email
- treat other contacts you may be given with discretion.

Exercise 10: the information interview

Try out an information interview. Practise the technique on a friend or colleague first if you wish. Some questions to ask include:

- What does the job involve on a day-to-day basis?
- Where does it fit in with the rest of the organization?
- Are there significant changes going on in the job or the organization?
- What skills and knowledge are most important in the job? (Remember to ask about general skills, like using computer databases or team-working, as well as job specific skills and knowledge.)
- Are any qualifications required/preferred? Are any particular courses or institutions seen as better than others in this field?
- What training or development is available in this job?
- What are the career backgrounds of job holders? What experience do you need to have?
- How does recruitment work in this job/occupation/sector and what are the most important selection criteria and behaviours they look for?
- When people leave or move on, where do they go?
- Are there likely to be vacancies in the short term and longer term?

Using people you already know to help you find your way to people with the information and advice you need is an important part of career planning. Such 'networking' has always been important in types of work where jobs are fluid and often not formally advertised. As the whole labour market becomes more fluid and fast-moving, networking is increasingly important to us all.

Summary

Today you have researched your career options by:

- defining your information needs
- mapping possible career paths
- identifying information sources
- learning how to use information interviews

Before you move on, check that the information you have gathered has been summarized on the charts you drew up for each of your career options at the start of this chapter.

Adopting this purposeful approach to finding out about your job options may feel like hard work. But it is likely to save you a lot of time, money and energy by making it more likely that you apply for jobs which you actually want and know about and make wiser choices in the qualifications you study for.

The work you have done today also equips you with some of the most important career planning skills: knowing how to get information and also how to judge its reliability.

Now we have completed the second building block of career planning – understanding jobs. We are ready to go on to the third and final stage of career planning – making choices and taking action.

Remember if you are not happy with any of the career options you have generated so far, you can go back to the options thinking stage and try again.

SUNDAY

MONDAY

TUESDAY

WEDNESDAY

THURSDAY

FRIDAY

SATURDAY

Questions

Questions to check your understanding

1. The work environment and job content of a career option tell you:
   a) How much you would be paid ❏
   b) What qualifications would be required ❏
   c) What this option would really feel like ❏
   d) What hours you would work ❏

2. Most employers see qualifications as:
   a) Less important for higher skill jobs ❏
   b) Of little importance in selecting the most suitable recruits ❏
   c) More important than experience ❏
   d) An indicator of some of the knowledge and skills you have ❏

3. The most useful person to have an information interview with is:
   a) Someone who has recently done the kind of job you are exploring ❏
   b) A friend ❏
   c) A work colleague or someone you are studying with ❏
   d) A much more senior person who did the job a long time ago ❏

Questions to capture your reflections

1. If you have done some information interviews, what have you learnt about how to get the best out of them?

2. Are any of your career options in jobs or organizations which are changing significantly? How will this change affect those jobs?

3. The websites I have found most useful in exploring my career options are... Why?

4. How easy has it been to find out about likely levels of career opportunities in your options? What factors have you been looking out for?

5. Has finding out more about your options changed your mind about which might be more or less interesting to do on a daily basis?

6. Mapping the possible career paths into some of my work options has helped me see that...

7. Do you have the necessary qualifications to pursue all of your options? If not, which courses do employers favour for options where you will need to study?

FRIDAY

Making choices

The main task for today is to pull together what you have learnt so far this week, so you will want your notebook handy to review your answers to the exercises and to look at the notes you have made. The aim is to examine how the career options you have researched measure up with your values and interests and whether they meet your personal requirements. You also need to consider how well your skills, knowledge and experience match up with those demanded by your options, and whether opportunities are likely to be available.

There are a number of choices that have to be made in order to achieve a better sense of career direction. As you make choices you are opening some doors but closing others. Some doors can be reopened in the future but not always without cost, which is one reason why today's work on your choices is so critical.

Our goal is that by the end of today you should have a much clearer sense of direction, so that you can move on to taking action. This means that there are a number of important questions that you must try to answer today. Most importantly, you must try to decide whether you have identified some career options that are both *attractive* and *achievable*.

Many career plans will involve skill development, and in the final part of this chapter, we will review how to go about accessing development opportunities at work or through education.

Pulling together what you have found out

By now you should have identified several possible career options and researched them in some depth. The stages in deciding between your various options involve:

- deciding how attractive they are by comparing them with your work values and work interests
- reviewing the impact of any factors or lifestyle issues that may constrain your choice of options
- deciding how achievable each option is for you by comparing your options with your skills, knowledge and experience, and levels of opportunity
- weighing the pros and cons of each option.
- determining your overall preference between options.

Start by trying to decide how attractive the options are to you. First, gauge the extent to which each option matches up with your work values.

Comparing options with your work values

One way to do this is to review each of your options against your self-rating of work values (Exercise 1). Consider the three work values that you identified as most important and ask for each of your possible career options:

Will the work involve this value? (Answer YES or NO)

- How does each option score? It is worth rating your current job as well (if you have one).
- How do the options compare? Will they satisfy the values that are most important to you?

If your options satisfy values that are not important to you, it may not matter. For example, the fact that an option is likely to provide a high salary or a friendly work environment is not going to put most of us off. However, you may be trying to avoid work that involves certain work values – risk, for example. You should also consider whether your values will clash with those of a potential employer.

Comparing options with your work interests

You have already identified your profile of work interests. Now you need to see whether your options are likely to involve activities that interest you. If you have researched your options thoroughly you will now know something about what they involve.

One way to do this is to construct a profile for each of your options in just the same way that you constructed a profile for yourself. You can do this by going back to Exercise 2, where you rated yourself, and use the same framework to rate each option in turn.

For each option, ask the question:

Does this option provide opportunities for ...?

Use the 1 to 5 scale giving scores from 1 = an option that will provide no opportunity for this activity to 5 = an option that will provide plenty of opportunity for this activity.

Now you can compare your own score profile from Exercise 2 with that of each of your options using the same six types of work interests:

	Exercise 2 *My interests*	**Option 1**	**Option 2**
Highest			
Second			
Third			

You can easily add in extra options as columns on the chart. Some key questions are:

- Are the two highest activity areas for each of your options the same as or different from those that you found you preferred?
- Are all your possible options scoring highly in the same interest areas?
- How do your options compare with your current job?

What do you learn from this? How attractive are your options to you? Are they the sorts of jobs that you would enjoy? How do they match up with your real priorities?

At this stage you may be in one of three different situations.

1. **Options match interests and values.** You are ready to go on and see how you measure up against your options in terms of skills, knowledge and experience.
2. **Options match interests and values to some extent.** Should you go back and review your options? Can you think of any other options that you ought to consider? Or have you changed your mind about your interests and values?
3. **Options do not seem to match up with interests and values.** More work is required. Review your values and interests. You

may also want to review your options. It may be helpful to ask someone else for a second opinion (friends, work colleagues, family). You should not expect to make your career plan on your own, so this may be a good time to involve someone else.

It is possible that you are not yet ready to make a career plan. You may need to do more work on the first two building blocks of the career planning process – *learning about self* or *learning about jobs*. See the Guide to resources at the back of the book for additional sources of information. This includes materials that can be used to help in learning about yourself.

Practical constraints

In assessing the overall attractiveness of different options, remember the practical constraints on your work choices, which we looked at on Thursday. How do you want work to fit in with the rest of your life?

- **Working patterns:** How much time do you wish to give to your work? Are you constrained by domestic and caring responsibilities, or other activities and interests? For example, do you wish to work part-time or term time only?
- **Flexible working:** How important is it that you have some flexibility in your work? Do you want to be able to do some work from home or to work flexible hours?
- **Work location:** How far are you prepared to travel to work? Are you willing to move house? Would you like to work from home?
- **Pay and benefits:** Will your requirements for pay and other benefits be met?

Comparing options with your skills, knowledge and experience

A key purpose of our research into possible options has been to find out their demands in terms of skills, knowledge and experience. You should now be able to use the information generated about your skills, knowledge and experience to determine how well you match with each of your possible options.

You may need to go back and look at the results of Exercises 6 and 8 to check whether the skills and knowledge you currently possess match up with those of your job options.

Skills and knowledge are often acquired through education. Are there qualifications that people doing these jobs are expected or required to have? *Do you, or are you about to, have them?*

Are there other skills or knowledge that are necessary to do this job? Can you provide evidence that you have acquired these skills and/or the relevant knowledge?

Do you have the necessary experience to convince someone that you can do the job? Do you feel you have the experience, but would find it difficult to convince someone that it is really relevant? Alternatively, should you be thinking about how you are going to get the experience?

For most types of career option, you will find yourself in one of three situations.

1. *You already have the skills, knowledge, qualifications and experience required.*

Next step: choosing options prior to action planning.

2. *You have most of the skills, knowledge, qualifications and experience required.*

Next step: think how you might acquire the additional skills, knowledge, qualifications or experience needed. Key steps are to:

● do more research to find out how people acquire the sort of experience you need. What jobs do they do? Can you get one of those jobs?

- consider going ahead with your action planning, on the assumption that you believe you can access the development you need. The issue of access to development is considered in the later sections of this chapter.

3. *You currently lack the skills, knowledge, qualifications and experience required.*

Next step: review the possibilities for acquiring the skills, knowledge, qualifications or experience needed before you can pursue your desired career option.

It is really important to be clear for each of your options which situation you are in as this affects what you do next.

Comparing options with likely levels of opportunity

Using the labour market information you have collected, you need to make a judgement about the likely level of opportunity, both now and in the future, for each option. Are they in fields that are expanding or contracting?

Choosing a preferred option

At this stage, try to make an overall judgement between the different options you have been considering. Before doing that there are a few points to consider.

- Do you have a plan B as well as a plan A? If your preferred choice was impossible, what would you do?
- Are your options extending your future work possibilities or closing them down? Remember that work is changing continuously and we must plan for future change
- Do your possible options feel right to you? Are you looking forward to them? If not, rethink your choices.

The next exercise aims to help you become clearer about your preferences between your different options. Ideally, there should be a good fit between your preferred options and yourself. In practice, you may have to compromise.

Your decision should be based on the extent to which options:

- cater for your interests, values and any constraints or lifestyle issues
- are within reach of your skills, knowledge, qualifications and experience
- have sufficient levels of opportunity.

Exercise 11: preferences between career options
You may find it helpful to rate each of your career options on the following scales:

Attractiveness		**Ideal**
Values	0	10
Interests	0	10
Constraints/Lifestyle	0	10
Achievability		
Skills/Knowledge	0	10
Qualifications	0	10
Experience	0	10
Opportunities	0	10
Overall rating	0	10

- How do your options compare?
- Do you have a preference for one option?
- Which option presents the best combination in terms of attractiveness and your ability to achieve it?

Accessing development

Your preferred career option may be in itself a return to full-time education or training; in this case you will have already started thinking about possible courses. However, the need for further skill development is common to many career plans. Development may involve:

- an educational course (full/part-time or distance-learning)
- training at work (through on-the-job coaching or training courses)
- a job move or project which gives you the experience you require to get closer to your career goal.

While taking a course or accessing development can be done at any age and, even though age discrimination is illegal in the UK, informal barriers can exist. People often still have expectations that certain things should be done by a certain age. There are many reasons why this is an unrealistic attitude nowadays but it can be harder for older people to get access to some education or development opportunities. However, being clear about why you want to do a particular course and its benefits is one way of improving your chances.

In this section we look at how to access development, in the form of both educational courses and development at work.

Educational courses

In many ways going back to education is getting easier. The range of colleges and courses is expanding, and prospectuses are easily available. The internet gives access to a huge amount of detailed information on education. There are many part-time courses and we can also study from home (through so-called 'distance-learning'). However, we also have to realize that competition for places on some courses is stiff and the

SUNDAY

MONDAY

TUESDAY

WEDNESDAY

THURSDAY

FRIDAY

SATURDAY

costs of education can be high. Educational qualifications cannot guarantee you the job you want, although the right qualification will improve your chances of success.

Before choosing a course, you will need to identify what *level of qualification* might be appropriate. On Thursday we related levels of qualifications to levels of jobs. We can think of levels in terms of academic qualifications (GCSE, A-level, degree, professional and postgraduate qualifications) but there are also many vocational qualifications, such as apprenticeships. The UK has a unified system of classifying vocational qualifications (NVQs) by broad level. Having the right qualifications is essential for many jobs and formal professional accreditation is required to work in some fields. Colleges and employers can advise you on the appropriate level of course to aim for, or the educational path to take through several courses.

Other aspects of courses to clarify are:

- subject or subject mix, curriculum and options
- key skills taught as part of the course (e.g. computer skills)
- location of colleges
- full-time, part-time or distance-learning options
- entry qualifications required
- precise qualification awarded

- recognition of course, if relevant, by professional body or employers
- length of course
- opportunities to gain work experience (e.g. placements, block releases)
- facility to change course if desired
- fees and availability of grants/sponsorship
- special government or industry schemes
- pattern of terms and hours of attendance
- teaching methods and staff/student ratios
- methods of assessment (e.g. exam, coursework).

Career development processes at work

Most of the development we gain in our working lives happens on the job or near to it. Your job research may have already given you clear ideas about job moves you need to make for development reasons. However, development at work will not just fall into your lap. You will need to understand the processes used by employers to develop their staff, and learn to use those processes to gain access to the training and job moves you need.

Personnel management, often called Human Resources or HR, has its own jargon and the diagram later in this section shows some of the processes we should try and find out about. We need to know:

- what each process is used for: how it affects the jobs people get and the training they receive
- whether we can use the process to obtain career information, send signals to the organization about what we want to do or have a better dialogue about possible options.

Four important types of use shown in the diagram are: **assessment, job-filling, development** and **career planning**. Processes can have more than one use. For example, an appraisal interview can be used to assess (openly or secretly), to discuss career plans, and to identify training and development needs. The output of this appraisal may influence whether the person being appraised is eligible to apply for jobs and whether he or she is selected.

Some processes are used primarily for **assessment**: identifying our strengths and weaknesses. Appraisal of performance and/or potential by a manager is the commonest, but larger organizations may also use assessment centres. These consist of a series of tests, exercises and interviews applied to a group of people often over two or three days. These may act as the gateway to a particular job level (e.g. senior management) or special development programmes.

The processes for **filling jobs** are crucial but often elusive. You will need to understand how vacancies are notified, what the selection criteria are for the jobs you want, and how the selection process really takes place. Company intranets are now often used to advertise and apply for internal vacancies. If skill criteria (e.g. communications, teamworking) are specified for jobs they can give you clues to the skills you need to show you have.

Informal influence and networking are often important in making internal job moves. You need to establish who takes short-listing and selection decisions, and who they are likely to consult about candidates, so you can gently raise your profile in the right quarters.

A range of processes combine planned job experience and development. These include development schemes or high potential or 'talent' programmes. Succession plans, still sometimes secret, plan possible job moves for some individuals. Project assignments and secondments give valuable development. Other **training and development** processes include formal or informal coaching, learning sets, off-the-job training and facilities for sponsorship.

As the trend to self-development has taken root, newer processes, such as career workshops, are aimed at helping **career planning.** Development centres combine assessment with development planning. Career or Learning resource centres contain career and training information, as do intranet sites. Mentoring puts employees in touch with someone more senior who can help them develop their career. Peer support through buddying is also quite common.

Learning to understand and play the system using these processes can be vital to us achieving our own career goals. Understanding career processes comes from a mix of reading formal descriptions (increasingly on company intranets) and informal discussions with colleagues.

Finding a manager or work colleague to talk to about both how careers work in this organization and your own career can be really helpful. It is important that you look for someone you can trust and who will be straight with you and not just 'spin' the corporate line. Some organizations will allocate you a mentor who will take on this role but more often this is something you will have to initiate yourself. This is another important way that informal processes and networking in the workplace can help you achieve your career goals.

It is worth reviewing your own experience of getting development at work. Which of these processes have you used and which might you use in the future? What would help or hinder you doing this? Making a list in your notebook will enable you to check back and review your experience at a later date.

Summary

Today you have:

- examined your career options against your values, interests and skills
- chosen one or more career options to form the basis of your action plan
- identified educational courses you may need
- looked at how you might use development processes at work

We have outlined a systematic way of reviewing all the information you have gathered to enable you to become clearer about your preferences so that you can choose the career plan you want to take forward. Sometimes, you will realize at this stage that there is more than one viable option and that you need to explore each option further.

Decisions can't always be made without getting some real experience. Jobs and careers do not always turn out as expected. New opportunities arise and we find that we are good at or enjoy some things that we had not expected to and vice versa. Career plans should be changed or adapted as we gain new experiences.

Very often even when you have a preferred option, you will realize that you could improve your chances of achieving it if you had more knowledge or experience of exactly what this option involves. This is something we will discuss further on Saturday.

SUNDAY
MONDAY
TUESDAY
WEDNESDAY
THURSDAY
FRIDAY
SATURDAY

Questions

Questions to check your understanding

1. Having a clear sense of direction is important:
   a) For a good lifestyle ❏
   b) For deciding what job you want ❏
   c) So you can move on to taking action ❏
   d) Before you ask anyone for information or support ❏

2. Understanding development processes at work is necessary to:
   a) Appear keen to get on ❏
   b) Get access to training and job moves ❏
   c) Meet the right people ❏
   d) Keep up appearances ❏

3 Career options need to be:
   a) Attractive and achievable ❏
   b) A challenge ❏
   c) Within easy reach ❏
   d) Have plenty of opportunities ❏

Questions to capture your reflections

1. The career options I have identified that are both attractive and achievable are...
2. What are the pros and cons of each of these options?
3. The way I have checked that these options will fit with the rest of my life is...
4. Are there practical constraints that may affect your choices? If so, what are they?
5. What do you need to learn to get to where you wish to go and how will you acquire the additional skills, knowledge or experience you need?
6. Do some of your options need much more investment in training and education than others? How do you feel about this?
7. I have tested the realism of my career plan by...

SATURDAY

Taking the first steps

Now that you have identified some possible career options, you need to set about producing an action plan to make your vision of the future a reality. This may involve quite small changes in your current job or in your life outside work; or it may be a major upheaval including a change of job, employer and location or re-entry into education. Some action plans will therefore be quite simple while others may involve a commitment to several years of retraining and change to get to where you want to be. Making such a major change is like embarking on a journey where you may not know exactly where you will end up because things will happen on the way that may affect your plans. Whatever your situation, you need to clarify and schedule your actions in relation to each option you are considering. Today we will be examining how these first steps are taken:

- clarifying types of action required
- preparing to present yourself through CVs, application forms and interviews
- applying for jobs and courses
- getting support
- setting goals and a timetable
- monitoring progress

Clarifying types of action required

Earlier we identified some of the main kinds of career options as:

- changing the content of your current job
- moving to a job for which you already have the skills (this could be with your current employer or elsewhere)
- moving to a job requiring further training or job experiences (again, with your current employer or elsewhere)
- making a major career change into a new area of work, often requiring new qualifications
- other changes (e.g. return to full-time education, self-employment, voluntary work, moving geographically).

This way of looking at options can be helpful when you come to consider the main focus of your career action plan. Typical actions may include:

- renegotiating the content of your current job
- applying for jobs inside your own organization
- external job search
- accessing training or development at work
- applying for educational courses
- exploring other options and changes outside work.

Career options

Typical actions	Change within job	Job move	Job move needing training	Major career change	Other options
Renegotiate present job	✓				
Internal job search		✓	✓	✓	
External job search	✓	✓	✓	✓	✓
Development at work			✓	✓	
Education	✓			✓	✓
Other changes		✓	✓	✓	✓

97

Some career options are more likely to require each of these types of action than others, as suggested by the ticks in the boxes on the action planning grid shown above. You can use this grid to think through the main focus of your action plan. Remember that changes to your life outside work can also be identified and recorded in your action plan.

It is quite normal for a plan to involve different strands at this stage. So the first task is to identify the actions associated with each of the career options you are considering. Once you have identified the main action areas for each option, then you can move on to think about what is needed to put your plan into action. Usually this involves both getting support from other people and persuading someone, often a potential employer, to offer you a job. We start by looking at how to market yourself.

Marketing yourself

One of the major hurdles in getting the sort of job you want is the selection process. This requires you to convince a potential employer that you are the right person for the job. Even if you are planning to be self-employed, you will have to convince potential customers or financiers of the viability of your venture. Essentially, you have to look at marketing yourself as though you were a product.

How do you market yourself?

The first thing you must know if you are going to be successful in the job hunt is why you want the job. Primarily, this is about understanding your own motivation for applying. If you really understand your work interests and values, you will be in a good position to do this.

Second, you must be able to convince your customer, in this case your potential employer, that you have the skills that they require. Once again, the work you have already done on reviewing your skills, knowledge and experience should be of help here.

In what ways will you have to market yourself?

Almost always you will have to write about yourself. This is one element of building your own career story. Either you will have to fill in an application form, or you will have to prepare a curriculum vitae (CV) that summarizes your work history. Many organizations now conduct the initial application stage in electronic form via the internet or e-mail.

Second, you will usually have an interview with your potential employer. Almost everybody wants to meet someone they will be working with. This also applies to job moves within your current employing organization.

Frequently, there are other components to a selection process. For example, there may be tests and presentations that have to be completed, or an assessment centre to attend. You might be asked to bring along examples of your work, or be required to provide the names of people who can give you a reference.

An important preparatory task is to work out what the employer is looking for. What selection criteria will they be using? Often it is more than just your knowledge and skills that are being assessed but how you behave and aspects of your personality as well. Employers are frequently interested in your interpersonal skills, especially if you will be working with clients or customers. When jobs are advertised this information is often included as part of the further particulars or in the job description. In other situations, this is something you should have identified in your research.

Many selection processes involve taking tests and sometimes these are done online as part of the screening process. If you have not taken a test for a while, it is a good idea to put in some practice. Lack of familiarity with taking tests can put you at a serious disadvantage, but a little practice can make all the difference and improve your performance considerably. In particular, are your Maths skills rusty? Do you know how to calculate a percentage? Examples of many types of test are available online either from leading employers or test publishers.

Many employers now also use 'situational' tests where you either have to describe how you would behave in a particular situation (e.g. handling an emergency situation at work), or have to rate the appropriateness of alternative courses of action in a given situation. Assessment centres also often involve group discussions and in all these types of test, employers are looking to see whether you would behave in ways that they consider appropriate. If you are unfamiliar with these aspects of the selection process, practice tests are available online.

It is important to realize that selection procedures often involve a number of stages, and the employer is effectively weeding out applicants at every stage of the process. This means that you must give each aspect of the selection process your best shot. There will be no second chance. Education and training providers also use similar procedures.

You should also be aware that, in general, selection procedures, particularly those used by major employers, are becoming more rigorous. There are several reasons for this. They include a greater concern for fairness, that is, not to discriminate against applicants unfairly. There is also a desire at all costs not to select people who will be unable to do the job required. The cost in time and money of running selection procedures is also an important factor for many employers.

Putting something down in writing

This is usually the first stage. Even in the most informal selection process, it will usually pay to have a CV prepared that you can hand over.

The main difference between completing an application form and writing a CV is that with an application form it is the employer who has decided what questions to ask; with a CV you have to decide what information to present to an employer about yourself.

What should it look like? It is best to avoid a handwritten CV, which may not look very professional. Most of us now have our CV on a computer which makes it easy to adapt each time we use it.

The CV should be broken down into sections just like an application form. These should include:

- personal background information: name, address, sex, etc.
- educational and professional qualifications: name of school/college attended, subjects studied, highest level of qualifications obtained, dates, etc.
- employment history: list of jobs (including job title, employer, dates of employment), responsibilities, key work experiences and achievements
- skills and knowledge: particular skills (especially those relevant to this application), including general skills such as computer and interpersonal skills
- current/last job: job title, name and address of employer, dates of employment, salary
- other relevant information: e.g. achievements outside paid employment
- names of referees: name, title and address for two people who would write you a reference (they should have been asked before you give details).

The exact form a CV should take will vary considerably between jobs and labour markets and needs to be adapted accordingly. If you were planning to become a university professor, your CV would list all the research you had done, the journal articles and books you had written, your teaching experiences, and so on; it might fill 20 pages. For most other jobs two or three pages will normally be sufficient.

As selection processes have become more sophisticated, so have CVs. The trend currently is to include in your CV a few headlines or bullet points that sum up some key points about you and what you have to offer. This is an opportunity to highlight skills or experiences that are then expanded upon in the rest of the CV. The CV should be more than just a record of what you have done, and bring out what you have learnt (skills, knowledge) on the way. It needs to be adapted and focused for each job application.

It is usual also to include with your CV a covering letter or email outlining your reasons for applying and emphasizing which of your skills and experiences are relevant to the position. This is an important opportunity to expand on the factual information contained within your CV.

You may not be able to complete some sections of a CV or an application form because, for example, you are only just leaving university and have never had a job.

Similarly, you should give less emphasis to things that happened a long time ago than to your more recent achievements, but always explain any gaps in your employment record.

Hints for application forms

Print or make a copy of the form before you begin and make detailed notes of what information you are going to put in each section, especially for open-ended questions. Now that most forms are electronic, you should complete the form as a draft and then ask someone else to have a look at it before you finalize and submit the actual form.

Keep a copy of the completed form so that you have a record of what you wrote about yourself. Check over this before you go to an interview. This is especially important if you are applying for several jobs as you need to remember what you said to each potential employer.

Nowadays most forms are completed electronically but some may still be designed to be filled in by hand. Pay attention to any special instructions about how to complete an application form. Does it say use black ink? (The form may well be photocopied, so black or dark blue are usually the best colours to use.) Have you used capital letters (e.g. for surname), when requested to do so? Presentation counts for more than it used to; write neatly and check (or get someone else to) that your spelling is correct.

If you are applying for jobs where there will be hundreds of applicants, be mindful that getting any of these little details wrong might result in the rest of your application never being read. The first sift of a pile of application forms is frequently just to check that they have been completed correctly. Perhaps just 30 seconds is allocated to your form. Some applicants fail at this hurdle.

Don't lie! It may catch up with you and will almost certainly mean you lose the job. How is the employer to know that this is the only lie you have told them?

Answers to questions on application forms should always be written concisely. However, sometimes there will not be sufficient space to write in all that is relevant. In this case it is normally appropriate to use a continuation sheet. Such sheets should always have your name on, and should specify to which section of the form they apply.

Don't leave questions unanswered; write 'None' or 'Not applicable'. Think carefully about doing this, as too many answers like this could create a negative impression.

Some employers now concentrate on looking for evidence of key skills, and the ability – or 'competence' – to cope with particular aspects of the job. So, for example, an application form might ask how you would deal with a difficult customer.

Or it might ask you about your own experience of handling difficult people. Answer such questions as fully and clearly as you can. They are likely to be a critical part of your application.

Presenting yourself at interviews

Research and preparation are vital. This means thinking about questions you might be asked and preparing your answers. It also means thinking carefully about what information you want to be sure you get across.

You should also research your potential employer before going for an interview. Interviewers expect you to know about the organization and be able to tell them why you would like to work for them in particular.

If you haven't had a job interview for a long time it is a good idea to rehearse. The best way to do this is to get a friend, colleague or partner to interview you. Failing that, practise speaking your replies out loud.

Make notes of key points. Prepare possible answers for difficult questions.

Interviewers want applicants to talk; try to avoid one-word answers. *'Have you had experience of...'*? Answer: 'Yes, when I worked at...we did...' *or* 'No, but at... we did...'

As well as answering the interviewer's questions, it is appropriate sometimes to add a few points about yourself that you think are especially important for the interviewer to know about.

Getting support

Once we are committed to making some changes in our working lives – however modest – we need to discuss our plans with other people. In some cases, for example with friends, this has the function of helping us check out whether our plans seem sensible to other people who know us. We may also get help from our friends in tackling the job market through their knowledge and networks of contacts. We talked about using networks in relation to collecting information on your work options. The same people may help you find out about specific vacancies and recruitment processes.

When it comes to families, some career plans may simply require their emotional support, for example in seeking a change in the content of a current job. Other options (e.g. a radical job move, a relocation or a return to education) have profound implications for other family members. These are clearly family decisions and need very careful discussion.

Broaching the subject of career change at work can be quite difficult. How you deal with your manager and colleagues will depend on whether you think they are likely to be supportive and whether you need their help in moving job or accessing development.

Think too about how you can give yourself support. A major career change can be a very upsetting event to contemplate. You may feel frightened and uncertain. If you are job seeking after redundancy, or trying to return to work after a long period at home, you may face many setbacks before you achieve your goal. You need to think how to keep your spirits up and give yourself a reward for successful steps along the way.

If you are finding it very difficult to identify a satisfactory option, or to find the job you are looking for, there are other sources of support or professional help you can turn to, including:

● career services: both general ones and those for students and former students of educational institutions
● job clubs set up for job hunters to get together
● career counsellors or career coaches.

Some professional bodies also provide useful information about careers in their field. For more information on such resources, see the Guide to resources given at the back of this book.

Setting goals and a timetable

Now it is time to try to list some of the specific goals or actions you need to take to pursue your preferred career option. This is, in essence, your career plan.

Your plan will often be a mixture of short-term and longer-term actions. For example, if the teacher we thought about earlier decides to write books from home, the list (with timetable) might include:

- sort out a small working space (this week)
- find another parent who will 'swap' childcare occasionally to cover travel in set-up phase (this month)
- map out three or four good ideas for books. Work one up in some detail (next two months)
- identify three most likely publishers and write to them (next two months).

In this case she/he is likely to know within a few months how feasible this plan is, and will either persist with it or adopt a different short-term goal (e.g. supply teaching) while thinking again.

The young accountant we thought about might decide to:

- give current employer at most one more year to signal promotion intentions
- approach an appropriate senior partner and ask for some informal mentoring support (this month)
- meanwhile make contacts in two or three larger companies expanding in Europe (six months)
- get CV up-to-date (this month)
- start working on improving rusty French (next month).

If your plan includes looking for other jobs, then it is better to focus on making a small number of very thoughtful approaches to employers rather than sending off hundreds of standard letters. Make sure you know how these employers notify vacancies and fill jobs. Only go for jobs which really are an improvement on your current situation or take you in the direction you want to go. Many of us work in highly specialized labour markets and it is important to understand just how the employers we are interested in working for recruit.

If you have not changed job for a long time or are planning to move into a new field of work, you will need to allow more time for research and preparation than if you have been applying for jobs recently. In setting a timetable you should also bear in mind the amount of effort involved in each action, and when you will fit these activities in. Goals should be challenging but achievable. Discussing your goals and timescale with someone else can help you to ensure they are realistic.

Exercise 12: your career plan

I'D LIKE TO BE EUROPEAN SALES MANAGER BY NEXT MONTH. WHAT D'YOU THINK?

Make a list of some practical goals and actions for each of the options you are considering. A simple list is likely to be more helpful than a very complex or elaborate one.

Next add in approximate timescales for achieving them.

Monitoring and adapting your plans

As with any planning process, career plans should be frequently monitored and reviewed. Are you doing the things you planned to do? If not, is the problem lack of motivation or shortage of time, or do you now think that the goal was inappropriate? Even more than other kinds of plans, career plans must not be seen as rigid and unchanging:

- They have no absolute timescales and direction may matter more than speed of progress.
- They will be affected by external events and must be modified accordingly.
- They depend wholly on your own desire for change and your determination not to let them fizzle out.

The key is to see career planning as a learning activity. We are learning more about the world of work and ourselves all the time. Sometimes a setback means that a goal will be achieved more slowly. Sometimes we learn that part of our plan will not work out, and we need to think again and modify our plan. Very often, our plans are conditional on labour market opportunities, and what we continue to learn about ourselves. For example, we often discover we have skills we did not identify at first.

You should not, therefore, feel that you have failed if you need to adapt your plans. What matters is that you use career planning to give yourself a direction, and the best chance of moving in this desired direction. As long as you are learning in this way and acquiring skills as you go, you are ensuring your future employability.

In fact responding to changing circumstances is a key skill in career planning. New experiences provide the opportunity to make new discoveries about yourself – about what you are good at and what you enjoy and also what you are not so good at and what you don't enjoy. Plans do need to change in the light of experience.

Career planning can be a challenging, sometimes uncomfortable, process. It can also be very hard work. However, if you don't do it, you are likely to end up at best dissatisfied and at worst unemployable. The choice is yours.

Summary

Today you have built on your earlier work of learning about jobs and about yourself. You have moved forward from your preferred career option to building a plan for action. This has included:

- types of action required
- marketing yourself through CVs, application forms and interviews
- setting goals and timescales
- monitoring and adapting plans

Putting a career plan into action is probably the hardest part of the process. Nevertheless, if you have done the first stages of learning about yourself and the world of work, you will be in a good place to move forward with your plans.

Plans do fall apart because the world changes, you change and/or your circumstances change. However, the advantage of well-made plans is that they should not lead to regrets. Life is unpredictable and plans have to be made on the basis of some best guesses about the future. Sometimes the unexpected will happen – businesses fold, reorganize or relocate and

SUNDAY
MONDAY
TUESDAY
WEDNESDAY
THURSDAY
FRIDAY
SATURDAY

people suddenly lose their jobs, but it could just as easily be an unexpected job or promotion opportunity that turns up.

Good career planning is really a set of processes for making career decisions that consider all the relevant aspects of your situation. Our aim has been to provide you with a framework for doing this.

So has the effort you have put into your career planning been of benefit to you? And have you acquired some understanding and skills which you can go on using in managing your own career?

Questions

Questions to check your understanding

1. Career plans:
   a) Can't be changed ❏
   b) Respond to changing circumstances ❏
   c) Do not need monitoring and reviewing ❏
   d) Should not be affected by external events ❏

2. You need to market yourself to:
   a) Convince an employer that you are the right person for the job ❏
   b) Make yourself feel good ❏
   c) Make yourself look interesting ❏
   d) Cover up any gaps in your CV ❏

3. It is good to talk to people about our plans:
   a) Because it makes life easier ❏
   b) So that our friends and family can help us find a job ❏
   c) Because change can be scary ❏
   d) To check out whether our plans seem sensible ❏

Questions to capture your reflections

1. The most important actions my career plan requires are: ...
2. I have prepared for the job hunting process by...
3. For one of your career options, what reasons have you identified for wanting this type of work?
4. For the same option, what examples of your experiences or achievements would persuade an employer that you will be good at this type of work?
5. The people who can help me with my next steps are: ...
6. My timetable for achieving the steps in my action plan is: ...
7. My strategy for coping with setbacks is: ...

SUNDAY | MONDAY | TUESDAY | WEDNESDAY | THURSDAY | FRIDAY | SATURDAY

Surviving in tough times

The career planning activities in this book will have helped you to clarify what you are looking for in a job but also what you offer to employers and how to put this across. In tough times, you need to build and maintain your employability, and the exercises and questions at the end of chapters will have highlighted your strengths and also your development needs. Having a flexible approach to career planning is especially helpful when times are tough, as are the tools for researching the particular parts of the labour market where you may want to work. Whether you are choosing to make a career move or are out of work, these tips will help you be well prepared in your hunt for your next job.

1 Put in focussed, well-researched job applications

Employers will be getting piles of applications whenever they advertise a job. Yours will stand out if it shows you have researched the organization and the job, and if you have bothered to make your CV and covering letter really relevant to what they are looking for. Fewer, better researched applications are more likely to bring you success.

2 Look for places where things are, or will be, better

Now might be the time to go somewhere you have always wanted to visit, and work there. The western, developed economies may be in a poor state but other countries are still growing rapidly and offer opportunities for those courageous enough to give it a go. You may also be able to find other sectors or types of work closer to home where your skills are relevant and opportunities are better. Pick options where future employment growth is likely – keep looking ahead.

3 Invest in your own development

A recession can be a good time to acquire the skills you hope to use when things are a bit easier. If you have been planning to go back to education to get higher level skills or if you have identified a course you need to redirect your career, then now might be the time to do it. If you are employed, look also for development opportunities in your current job. In tough times employers value people who will take on a challenge or use their initiative. It's good for you too.

4 Keep up your networking

People are the most help when things are tough. So do keep in touch with a wide range of people who can give you sound advice and alert you to possibilities. Use your contacts to widen your job search if necessary. Remember though, those you ask may be very busy and have their own worries, so use other people's time considerately and thank them properly. Consider what you can offer others to make your networking mutually beneficial.

5 Develop short-term and long-term ideas

In a recession we often have to take work in the short term which we know is not what we want for the long term. This is fine as long as you do not lose sight of your longer-term aspirations. Less than ideal short-term choices can still help you move in the right direction. If your longer-term career goals start to look really unattainable, it becomes a matter of whether it is better for you to keep trying or to have a more serious rethink.

6 Keep your eyes open for free help

There are often special kinds of support available in tough times for people who are unemployed or who are working in small businesses or who live in particular geographical areas and so on. Free advice is always worth considering and may be just what you need. If you have studied, find out if you are still eligible for career support from your college or university.

7 Keep your spirits up

The biggest challenge of all is to keep optimistic when there are few opportunities or when you get a lot of rejections. Your friends and family are likely to help you here. It's important to realise that it's not your fault when times are tough, but equally important that you do the best you can in a difficult situation. Reward yourself even for small steps in the right direction.

8 Get yourself on the radar

If you know there are employers you really want to work for, a recession can be a good time to get onto their radar. If they are willing, talk to someone in your chosen work area, pay a visit, offer a short period of work experience – whatever it takes for them to know who you are. When a job does come up, you will be at a considerable advantage if they already know quite a bit about you.

9 Consider volunteering

If you are finding it difficult to get the type of job you want or even just feeling stuck in your present job, look for an opportunity to volunteer. Whether it is working for a community-based organization or a charity, here or overseas, it will be an opportunity to learn new skills and meet new people. Volunteering roles often allow you to take on considerable responsibility for projects or people. You can also work in areas that are unlikely to be open to you as a new employee in most organizations. It will demonstrate that you have initiative, something that most employers value.

10 Join a job club

Most areas have job clubs, especially for people who are out of work for some time. A job club can be an important way to get practical help and meet a supportive network of people in a similar situation. It is useful to be able to share information and tips both about surviving in tough times and about finding work.

Answers

Sunday: 1c; 2b; 3d
Monday: 1b; 2d; 3a
Tuesday: 1a; 2b; 3a
Wednesday: 1a; 2b; 3b

Thursday: 1c; 2d; 3a
Friday: 1c; 2b; 3a
Saturday: 1b; 2a; 3d

Guide to resources

Some useful books for further reading and a selection of websites with information relevant to careers and career planning

Books

Bolles, R.N. *What Color is Your Parachute?* Ten Speed Press. Updated annually

Hawkins, P. (1999) *The art of building windmills: Career tactics for the 21st century*. Graduates into Employment Unit, University of Liverpool

Hopson, B. and Scally, M. (1999) *Build Your Own Rainbow: a Workbook for Career and Life Management*. Management Books 2000 Limited

Lees, J. (2010) *How to Get a Job You'll Love*. 6th Edition. McGraw Hill

Schein, E.H. (2006) *Career Anchors: Self Assessment*. 3rd Edition. Pfeiffer

Willis, L. and Daisley, J. (2006) *Springboard Women's Development Workbook*. 5th Edition. Hawthorn Press

Websites

Many employers and most educational institutions (and their alumni networks) can be found on the web. Some useful sites include:

UK higher education courses www.ucas.ac.uk

Graduate careers information, including career planning tools and information about studying abroad www.prospects.ac.uk

Information on careers, jobs, education and training https://nextstep.direct.gov.uk

Job seeking www.direct.gov.uk/en/Employment/Jobseekers/programmesandservices

Career planning and job hunting www.jobhuntersbible.com

Career weblinks www.careersa-z.co.uk

Career stories and ideas www.icould.com

Job clubs www.gbjobclubs.org

Recruitment agencies www.rec.uk.com/jobseeker

Social networking for work www.linkedin.com

International employment advice www.labourmobility.com

Other potential sources of information/advice/support

University and College Career Services
Job Centres/Employment Service
Professional associations
Sector Skills Councils
Chambers of Commerce

Notes

ALSO AVAILABLE IN THE 'IN A WEEK' SERIES

BODY LANGUAGE FOR MANAGEMENT • BOOKKEEPING AND
ACCOUNTING • CUSTOMER CARE • SPEED READING • DEALING WITH
DIFFICULT PEOPLE • EMOTIONAL INTELLIGENCE • FINANCE FOR
NON-FINANCIAL MANAGERS • INTRODUCING MANAGEMENT
• MANAGING YOUR BOSS • MARKET RESEARCH • NEURO-LINGUISTIC
PROGRAMMING • OUTSTANDING CREATIVITY • PLANNING YOUR
CAREER • SUCCEEDING AT INTERVIEWS • SUCCESSFUL APPRAISALS
• SUCCESSFUL ASSERTIVENESS • SUCCESSFUL BUSINESS PLANS
• SUCCESSFUL CHANGE MANAGEMENT • SUCCESSFUL COACHING
• SUCCESSFUL COPYWRITING • SUCCESSFUL CVS • SUCCESSFUL
INTERVIEWING

For information about other titles in the series, please visit www.inaweek.co.uk

ALSO AVAILABLE IN THE 'IN A WEEK' SERIES

SUCCESSFUL JOB APPLICATIONS • SUCCESSFUL JOB HUNTING
• SUCCESSFUL KEY ACCOUNT MANAGEMENT • SUCCESSFUL LEADERSHIP
• SUCCESSFUL MARKETING • SUCCESSFUL MARKETING PLANS
• SUCCESSFUL MEETINGS • SUCCESSFUL MEMORY TECHNIQUES
• SUCCESSFUL MENTORING • SUCCESSFUL NEGOTIATING • SUCCESSFUL
NETWORKING • SUCCESSFUL PEOPLE SKILLS • SUCCESSFUL
PRESENTING • SUCCESSFUL PROJECT MANAGEMENT • SUCCESSFUL
PSYCHOMETRIC TESTING • SUCCESSFUL PUBLIC RELATIONS •
SUCCESSFUL RECRUITMENT • SUCCESSFUL SELLING • SUCCESSFUL
STRATEGY • SUCCESSFUL TIME MANAGEMENT • TACKLING INTERVIEW
QUESTIONS

For information about other titles in the series, please visit www.inaweek.co.uk